Sleepless Nights
and
Baby Kisses

Alysha Castillo

BookLeaf Publishing

India | USA | UK

ISBN: 978-93-5744-990-8

First edition 2022

DEDICATION

To my biggest fans, Manuel, Gideon and Citlali.

ACKNOWLEDGEMENT

I'd like to thank all of my English teachers that first taught me about poetry and the art of writing poems. With their encouragement, I was able to create something beautiful.

A huge shout out to my mom, Cyndi, for igniting my love of reading at a very young age and a big thank you for taking the time to scrapbook all of my best work (including my poetry) from my school days.
I'm so grateful for my supportive husband, Manuel, for encouraging me to follow my passions and take the leap into this challenge.

Thank you to my children, Gideon and Citlali, who inspire me each and every day.

To Dad and Sharon, Josh, Kerryann, Benjamin, Mom and Mark, thank you for always being there for me!

Finally, thank you to BookLeaf Publishing. I never would have gotten back into poetry without this challenge.

PREFACE

When I was in high school, the poetry days in English class drove me crazy. The teachers always asked questions like, "Why did the author write this?" and "What did the author mean when he (or she) said this?" Don't get me wrong, I enjoyed reading the poetry but having to analyze it took the fun out of it. Then came the assignments where we got to write our own poetry. I really enjoyed this part! I still have the poems that I wrote in high school and love to go back and read them.

Since high school, I haven't really done anything artsy besides a little drawing until the COVID-19 pandemic. During the pandemic, artists shared their talents with the world and helped people everywhere to create art in their own homes. I started following acrylic painting tutorials and painted over a hundred paintings. I was also able to write, illustrate and print out a couple of children's books for my kids.

When I saw advertising for #thewriteangle writing challenge by BookLeaf Publishing, I knew that it was going to be my next art adventure.

I hope you enjoy my collection of poems.

What is a Mother?

A soft comfy bed
Kisser of bonked heads
A never ending milk bottle
The destination of a toddle
A convenient tissue
Resolver of issues
A tooth brusher
A bug crusher
A reader, a pleader
A feeder, a cheerleader
An answerer of "why?"
A baker of pie
A preacher, a teacher
A nearby reacher
A singer of songs
Hider of tongs
Righter of wrongs
On duty all the day long
What can't she do
For the people she grew?
Nothing's impossible
For this woman unstoppable.

Ten Little Toes

I see ten little toes
Peeking out from under
The drape in the corner
Tap tap tapping
Impatiently waiting
To be found.
A little face peeks out
Every other moment
Just to make sure
I'm still there
Still watching
Still loving
Still smiling
At her mischievous little grin
Her pride at having found
The perfect hiding place.

Dirty Dishes

Dishes, dishes
If I could count the wishes
That I've made
To have the endless supply stayed
There would be a million wishes
All about dirty dishes.

Soap Water + Air = Magic

What makes bubbles so magical?
Is it the rainbowy hues
Of pink, blue and yellow
The bright reflections
Of the lights all around
Is it the shimmers and sparkles,
The kaleidoscope colours
The fleeting beauty
Of tiny neon worlds?
These perfect spheres
Somehow contain
The imaginations,
The wishes and dreams
Of a child
They bring joy and colour
For a brief moment
And then...
They pop!
And all of those wishes
The dreams and hopes
Of little ones
Are sent

Into the universe
To bring a little wonder
To those who have forgotten
To stop and take some time
To enjoy the simple pleasures
Of life.

Songs of Devotion

It really is a miracle
How a song of devotion,
A sacred hymn,
Can penetrate the fog
Of daily distractions
Ease the stress
Of many little worries
Repel the pull
Of social media

The words lift my soul
From the depths
Of hopelessness
Into a higher place
Where peace resides
Where perspective changes
Where God is

The melody frees my heart
From the weight
I didn't realize
Was crushing it
The breaths
I hadn't noticed
Were laboured

Come easier
Like a massage
That releases the tension
I didn't know
I was carrying

The doctrines taught
Remind me
Of classes attended
Of sermons taught
Of knowledge shared
And build my faith
My testimony
My love of the gospel

The Holy Spirit felt
Brings a smile
To my face
Tears
To my eyes
Warmth
To my heart

These musical praises
They call to me
More than any
Half-heard talk
Rushed chapter read
Or sleepy prayer uttered

Righteous songs
Truly can be
Prayers
Unto heaven
And bring blessings
Whenever I take the time
To sing.

Anyone Can "Art"

There is just one thing
That separates
The artists
From the non-artists

You may say
I know this one
It's practice
Right?
Almost

You just have to try
Give it a whirl
Take a shot
Pick up a pencil
A paintbrush
A chisel
Open your mouth
Put your fingers on the keys

If it doesn't work out
Try again
Or try something else
There are so many
Different ways

To be
An artist

Draw
Paint
Write
Perform Music
Act
So many different ways
To create

Find your passion
And go from there
You may stick with it
For years
Months
Weeks
A day
And that's ok

If you were able
To create something
To express yourself
Then it was a success
Effort un-wasted
Time well spent.

Sleepless Nights and Baby Kisses

They say
The days can drag on
But the years fly by
And it's so true

There are days full
Of tantrums
Crying, yelling
Food flung
Slammed doors
Thrown toys
To name a few

Sleepless nights full
Of bad dreams
Wet sheets
Teething pain
Growing pains
Throw up
Empty water cups

These are the days

That feel neverending
Days I can't wait
Until nap time
So I can have some "me time"
Kind of...
Until bed time
So I can rest
Sort of...

But then
There are the days
That turn out
Quite the opposite
Full of giggles and laughs
Hugs and kisses
Shared toys
Made up jokes
Stories read
With my lap full of
My precious kiddos

There are the good nights
That start with stories and lullabies
I love yous
Sleep tights
And end with
Sleep.
All. Night. Long.

These are the days
That make it all
Worth it
The exhaustion
The lack of social life
Never having a minute alone
And yes,
That includes on the toilet
And so much more
That I can't even list
In part, because it would be
A very long list

And in part, because
The good times
Outshine the bad
The hard times fade
Into the back
Of my memory
And the good times?
They are framed
In lights
At the forefront
Of my thoughts

And all of the sudden,
Days turned into weeks
Months into years
One baby

(Who isn't a baby anymore)
Becomes two
(Who's also growing so so fast)

And I can't believe time
Has gone by
So quickly
Because it feels like
Just yesterday
That they were
Newborns

And I know
That even though
It's been hard
I'd do it all again
Because these little people
Are my greatest joys.

World's Best Dad

Their smiles
When you walk through the door
After work
Their little giggles
When you play peek-a-boo
Lali's little voice asking
Papa? Papa?
First thing in the morning
Gideon's love of the stories
You make up
Just for him
Your adorable selfies
With Lali
Smiling ear to ear
The look of pride
On Gideon's little face
When you tell him
That you're proud of him
When you do the
Elevator song
Again and again
Even though you're tired
When you laugh at Gideon's jokes
Even though you've heard them
A hundred times

When you are trying
To exercise
And he wants to too
So you let him join you
All these cute little moments
May not seem like much
To you
But to them
Each moment spent
With you
It's more proof
That they have
The world's best Dad.

Lamenting Limericks

The kids fell asleep in the car
I guess the trip was kinda far
At home they didn't nap
Poor me said "oh snap!"
For nap times my art sessions are.

Me and my big mouth
Can't seem to control what comes out
I oft am dismayed
At the things that I say
How I wish I could take them back.

We've again come down with a cold
This routine is getting old
At home we will stay
For six to ten days
While COVID has the world controlled.

Life-Changing Moments

There are moments in life
That happen so fast
Yet completely change
Your life

There's the moment
You know
You've found your soul mate
Your best friend that will stand by you
For eternity

When labour starts
And it really hits you
That the baby is here
That you're about to become
A parent

Baby's first steps
You can't believe
How fast time is going
And that your baby
Is not a baby anymore

When you witness
A car accident
And recognize
How close we are
To tragedy
At any given moment

When you feel
An earthquake
For the first time
And realize how powerful
And terrifying
Nature can be

When someone you know
Someone your age
Suddenly passes away
And you have to accept
You're not invincible
You never know when your time
Is up

Your first flight in an airplane
When you're 35 thousand feet high
And you feel
Like nothing is impossible

These moments
(And so many more)

They happen so fast
Yet completely change
Life as you knew it.

Poetry Therapy

I read some books of poetry
Seeking tips and tricks
I too would like to write a book
Made of my favorite picks

These books seemed to be quite dark
And really quite concerning
I started to feel sad
But the pages kept on turning

As I read page after page
I did begin to see
These poems not for me were written
Instead were therapy

There's something therapeutic
About putting into words
All that you may feel inside
How you see the world

I seem to have avoided
The pain and suffering
Many poets went through
While I sat wondering

Is there meat in meatloaf?
What outfit should I wear?
What would I do with all that money
If I were a billionaire?

I'm not sure how to end this poem
I could just keep on writing
I think I'll end it here though
So you can do something more exciting.

Trunk or Treat

I spent the afternoon
Thinking up ideas
Of games and things to do
For trunk or treat this year

I volunteered to be
The one to make it happen
If no one was appointed
To pull the planning wagon

I didn't want plan a dance
As most just stand around
Chatting with each other
Or just listening to the sound

I want it to be fun!
The kids will laugh and play
Doing things that interest them
It'll be the highlight of their day

Decorating pumpkins
A ball toss and cupcake walk
Feeding a hungry monster
Made of a cardboard box

A costume contest for the kids
Who dressed up will be good
But the part where they get candies
Is what they'll love most, I would!

Autumn Leaves

I love to see the autumn leaves
Change colours on the trees
They add a magic touch
To the new chill in the breeze

It marks the start of a new season
And gives us all a reason
To stop and take a minute
And see the significance within it

Change is part of life
It doesn't have to cause us strife
If we pick cheery over moody
It can bring our lives much beauty.

Forgotten Toast

There was a slice of bread
Chosen to make toast
So happy to leave it's bed
With the rest of the loaf

Into the toaster it went
To become all hot crispy
To a mouth it was to be sent
But minutes it waited: 150

Now there it sits
On the counter all alone
Waiting to be chewed to bits
Until to the trash it will be thrown.

How I Became an Artist

I've always wanted to be
Like the artists that I've seen
It seems to come so naturally
Having skills like that was my fantasy

I came across a painting class
A bear and aurora borealis
I bought it for my husband's birthday
And tried it on the replay

From then on I was hooked
All over the internet I looked
For beginner acrylic tutorials
I even bought quality materials

I started with Paris in the rain
All this painting kept me sane
I wasn't able to leave the house much as
The pandemic held the world in its clutches

I learned all about gradients
How to make my colours radiant

While working on the underpainting
Jesse's jokes were entertaining

Then come the top layers
And on canvases or papers
I could create a masterpiece
While my painting knowledge increased

Now I'm working on my own stuff
And whenever it gets tough
I look at all that I've accomplished
All that helped make me an artist.

Reading

Reading is an escape
Taking me to another world
Reading is a bubble
Blocking all outside problems from my mind
Reading is an adventure
Putting me in someone else's shoes for a while.
(2008)

Pizza Friday

I've never been very good
At deciding what to make
For dinner each and every night
It gives me a headache

I like to have a plan
Though it's a pain to write
It's nice to know ahead of time
So we can eat before it's night

My favorite thing to do
Depending on the food
Is plan the same thing each week
As long as it's something good

Many dishes I get bored
Of eating every week
It's good to have variety
Even if it's just a little tweak

Pizza however
Never will get old
It's always delicious
Even when it's cold

Every week it's a big hit
My 3-year-old boy knows
We eat pizza every Friday
He gets to punch the risen dough

We always make two different kinds
Hawaiian and Deluxe
We bake the dough from scratch
No need to pay big bucks

It tastes delicious and it's not greasy
Like the fast food pizzas are
I add a bunch of vegetables
It's healthier by far

I've never been very good
At deciding what to make
For dinner each and every night
But pizza is never a mistake.

Baby Talk

A child's growth
Is so neat to watch
Each stage
Brings new wonders
New challenges
New things to celebrate

Right now,
My baby girl
Is 16 months old
She's learning how to use words
To communicate
To make her desires known

She has included
Several words
In her vocabulary
Mama, Papá,
Diaper, Ball
Baby, Stop it
Bye bye, Uh oh
Milk, Shoes
And each day she learns more

The pride on her face

Is priceless
When we understand
What she's trying
To tell us
Her joy
Is contagious
And I can't help but smile
At her
And kiss her cute little cheek.

Mom Friends

In school, making friends was easy
But as an adult I have found
It's hard to make new friends
Especially when COVID had us home bound

On my travels and adventures
I've met many great ladies
But keeping in touch isn't easy
When you live in different countries

As a mom it's been easier
We meet at the playground
We have things in common
Though talk is hard while running around

I've made some cool mom friends
And it really is quite great
To have a chat together
While our kids enjoy a playdate

It's great to compare stories
Of the funny things kids do
And it's nice now and then
Having someone I can vent to

I value these friendships
Their worth is more than gold
I hope I can keep them
Until we are very old.

The World is Beautiful

Since I started painting
I've really started seeing
All of the world's beauty
That prove there's a supreme being

Breathtaking sunsets
Elegant flowers
Majestic mountains
I could stare at them for hours

Spectacular waterfalls
Noble trees
Puffy clouds
I imagine how I would paint these

In the beautiful sky above
I see perfect gradient
From blue and teal to red and orange
The colors are quite radiant

Flowers with their delicate petals
Present a challenge

I feel so very proud
When I'm able to capture their essence

I never have to worry
About what to paint tomorrow
I only need to look outside
And let the inspiration flow.

Big Brother

It's heartwarming to see
My baby boy
Step into the role
Of a big brother

Right from the start
He loved to give her
Hugs and kisses
And help out
By getting a clean diaper
Or a burp cloth

Now that they're a little older
I ask Gideon to watch Lali
While I run the trash out
Or take a quick shower
He does his best
To distract her
And comfort her if she cries
Then he tells me all about it
His little head held high

Of course they have
Their little squabbles
She plays with a favourite toy of his

He takes something out of her hands
She crumples a paper he's coloured on
He sits on my lap
(A spot she's very possessive of)

But the love that they have
For one another
Is strong
It shows in the sleepy hugs and kisses
As he's waking up from his nap
The songs he sings her
The silly things he does to make her laugh

It's heartwarming to see
My little boy
Rock the role
Of a big brother.